Join the FREE online
JACQUELINE WILSON
★ FAN CLUB ★

You can learn all about Jacqueline
from her monthly diary, her fan-mail
replies and her tour blogs.

There's also loads to discuss on the
message boards, you can customise your
page, have your own online diary,
put your picture into your favourite
Jacqueline book cover and don't forget
the competitions with incredible
prizes!

Sign up today at
www.jacquelinewilson.co.uk

THIS SUMMER HOLIDAY JOURNAL BELONGS TO:

HERE'S A PHOTO OF ME!

Name Ella-Boo Tait-Golden.

Address

Phone Number

Email

MY FAVOURITE HOLIDAY

I write a great deal about favourite holidays in *Jacky Daydream* and *My Secret Diary*. I loved going to the seaside, and the two most memorable holidays of my childhood were spent in Bournemouth and Newquay. I still like going to the seaside now – though the sea feels so freezing cold that I haven't got the courage to go in swimming any more. I like swimming in *warm* sea now! I recently had a fantastic holiday in Barbados where the turquoise water was just like jumping into a bath.

However, I think my all-time favourite holiday venue is Hay-on-Wye, which is nowhere near the sea. It's a tiny Victorian town in a valley on the Welsh Borders. It's magical countryside. There are gorgeous wild ponies up in the Black Mountains and you can see for miles if you stagger up the nearest Bluff. The River Wye runs beside the town and there are lovely riverside walks and a beautiful spot called the Warren for picnics and paddles in the water.

Hay has fantastic restaurants and pubs and a wonderful ice-cream parlour, so I always go home feeling very fat. But the best thing of all about Hay-on-Wye is the thirty second-hand bookshops – my idea of bliss!

By Jacqueline Wilson

MY FAVOURITE HOLIDAY

I had a lot of great holidays when I was a boy, but if I had to choose I'd pick the first time we went camping, when I was about to turn eleven.

We started off with a few days in the Lake District where we pitched our brand-new tents (one for Mum and Dad, one for my sisters and one for my brother and me) on a campsite overlooking Derwentwater, and I just couldn't believe how spectacular the view was, with the glistening lake and the mountains in the background. Then we drove over to Northumberland, visited Hadrian's Wall and had a lazy day or two by the sea.

Finally we went to stay with some friends who had a cottage in the Yorkshire Dales, but not big enough for everyone, so the boys still slept in the tent. I'd thought the lakes were impressive, but for me Swaledale was complete paradise, a truly beautiful, utterly peaceful valley with grass so green it was almost luminous, hidden away like a secret among the wild moors. We went for long walks alongside the River Swale or scrabbled up the side valleys to cook fry-ups, swim in rock pools and peer into the mouths of the ruined lead mine tunnels up there. I fell completely in love with the place and it's still my absolute favourite destination for a holiday!

By Nick Sharratt

♥ MY FAVOURITE ♥ HOLIDAY MEMORIES

What are your favourite memories from holidays? Maybe you went on an exciting trip abroad, relaxing on the beach and trying lots of lovely foreign food? Perhaps you made some new friends? Or your favourite holiday might have been spent at home, playing out in the sunshine, reading or doing lots of fun craft activities? Sometimes those are the best holidays of all!

_____

_____

_____

_____

_____

_____

_____

_____

_____

_____

_____

_____

_____

♥ MY DREAM ♥ HOLIDAY – AT HOME

Imagine you have the whole summer holiday ahead of you, free to do whatever you like. How would you spend your perfect holiday at home? You might read all your favourite books, try a new hobby like baking or keeping a scrapbook, or spend every minute in the garden or the park with your best friends!

_____
_____
_____
_____
_____
_____
_____
_____
_____
_____
_____
_____
_____
_____
_____
_____
_____

♥ MY DREAM ♥ HOLIDAY – ABROAD!

If you could go anywhere in the world, where would you go?
A romantic city like Paris? A hot beach in Spain?
How about seeing the sights in New York or Hollywood?
Picture your dream holiday abroad and the people you
would want to spend it with!

_____
_____
_____
_____
_____
_____
_____
_____
_____
_____
_____
_____
_____
_____
_____
_____
_____

♥ MY WORST ♥ HOLIDAY!

Have you ever had a holiday where everything went horribly wrong? Don't worry — everyone does! Write down your worst ever holiday experience, and why it was so bad!

Turkey

_____

_____

_____

_____

_____

_____

_____

_____

_____

_____

_____

_____

_____

_____

_____

♥ TOP TEN HOLIDAY ♥ DESTINATIONS

Write down the ten places you'd most like to visit on holiday – then, if you ever get the chance to go there, you can tick them off!

1. _____ ☐
2. _____ ☐
3. _____ ☐
4. _____ ☐
5. _____ ☐
6. _____ ☐
7. _____ ☐
8. _____ ☐
9. _____ ☐
10. _____ ☐

♥ MY PLANS FOR ♥ THIS SUMMER

If you already know how you're going to spend the summer, write down your plans here. If you don't, maybe you could list the things you *hope* you'll get to do instead!

♥ THE BOOKS I'LL ♥ READ THIS SUMMER!

With plenty of free time on your hands, summer is the perfect time to read lots of brilliant new books — and also to rediscover some of your old favourites! What will you be reading this summer?

Hopeully all
Jacqueline Wilson
books!

♥ ADDRESSES ♥

If you go away this summer you might want to write a postcard to your family and friends! Write their addresses down here.

Name _Abigail O'toob_

Address _I DK_

Phone Number _6666_ ~~8000~~

0811I I think.

Email _____

Name _____

Address _____

Phone Number _____

Email _____

Name _____

Address _____

Phone Number _____

Email _____

♥ ADDRESSES ♥

Name _____

Address _____

_____

_____

Phone Number _____

_____

Email _____

_____

Name _____

Address _____

_____

_____

Phone Number _____

_____

Email _____

_____

Name _____

Address _____

_____

_____

Phone Number _____

_____

Email _____

_____

♥ ADDRESSES ♥

Name _____

Address _____

_____

_____

Phone Number _____

_____

Email _____

_____

Name _____

Address _____

_____

_____

Phone Number _____

_____

Email _____

_____

Name _____

Address _____

_____

_____

Phone Number _____

_____

Email _____

_____

♥ ADDRESSES ♥

Name _____

Address _____

_____

_____

Phone Number _____

Email _____

_____

Name _____

Address _____

_____

_____

Phone Number _____

Email _____

_____

Name _____

Address _____

_____

_____

Phone Number _____

Email _____

_____

♥ QUICK ♥ HOLIDAY QUIZ!

1. In *Candyfloss*, which country does Floss's mum want the family to move to?

2. What is the capital city of Italy?

3. Who invites Biscuits to go on holiday with him in *Buried Alive*?

4. Tracy Beaker believes her mum lives abroad. In which famous city?   *Hollywood*

5. What is the tallest mountain in the world?

6. What country is Berlin the capital city of?

7. If you went to France, what sort of money would you need to take with you? Euros

8. In *Cookie*, Beauty and her mum go to Rabbit Cove. What's the name of the little cottage they stay in?

9. In *Cliffhanger*, Tim finds a girlfriend on holiday! What's her name?

10. When Gemma goes to visit Alice in Scotland in *Best Friends*, what present does she take her?

You can find the answers on the last page of the book!

JUNE

Mum and I had another lovely lazy morning
at Rabbit Cove and a picnic on the beach
— Cookie

1 JUNE

2 JUNE

3 JUNE

4 JUNE

5 JUNE

6 JUNE

7 JUNE

8 JUNE

9 JUNE

10 JUNE

11 JUNE

12 JUNE

13 JUNE

14 JUNE

15 JUNE

16 JUNE

17 JUNE

18 JUNE

19 JUNE

20 JUNE

21 JUNE

22 JUNE

23 JUNE

24 JUNE

25 JUNE

26 JUNE

27 JUNE

28 JUNE

29 JUNE

30 JUNE

JULY

I had sand in my hair and my ears and my mouth and even up my nose but I still didn't care – *Buried Alive*

1 JULY

2 JULY

3 JULY

4 JULY

5 JULY

6 JULY

7 JULY

8 JULY

Caboory world

Choco-
late

New clowthes

9 JULY

10 JULY

11 JULY

12 JULY

13 JULY

14 JULY

15 JULY

16 JULY

17 JULY

18 JULY

19 JULY

20 JULY

JULY

21 JULY

22 JULY

23 JULY

24 JULY

25 JULY

26 JULY

27 JULY

28 JULY

29 JULY

30 JULY

31 JULY

NOTES

AUGUST

I peeped out of the curtains, expecting to see
mountains and lochs and hairy Highland cattle
and men in tartan kilts – *Best Friends*

1 AUGUST

2 AUGUST

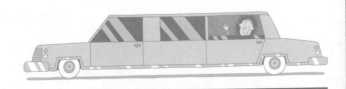

3 AUGUST

4 AUGUST

5 AUGUST

6 AUGUST

7 AUGUST

8 AUGUST

9 AUGUST

10 AUGUST

AUGUST

11 AUGUST

12 AUGUST

13 AUGUST

14 AUGUST

15 AUGUST

16 AUGUST

17 AUGUST

18 AUGUST

19 AUGUST

20 AUGUST

21 AUGUST

22 AUGUST

23 AUGUST

24 AUGUST

25 AUGUST

26 AUGUST

AUGUST

27 AUGUST

28 AUGUST

29 AUGUST

30 AUGUST

31 AUGUST

NOTES

SEPTEMBER

I saw us on a huge white beach, with kangaroos hopping across the sand and koalas climbing palm trees – *Candyfloss*

1 SEPTEMBER

2 SEPTEMBER

3 SEPTEMBER

4 SEPTEMBER

SEPTEMBER

5 SEPTEMBER

6 SEPTEMBER

7 SEPTEMBER

8 SEPTEMBER

9 SEPTEMBER

1O SEPTEMBER

11 SEPTEMBER

12 SEPTEMBER

13 SEPTEMBER

14 SEPTEMBER

15 SEPTEMBER

16 SEPTEMBER

17 SEPTEMBER

18 SEPTEMBER

19 SEPTEMBER

20 SEPTEMBER

21 SEPTEMBER

22 SEPTEMBER

23 SEPTEMBER

24 SEPTEMBER

25 SEPTEMBER

26 SEPTEMBER

27 SEPTEMBER

28 SEPTEMBER

29 SEPTEMBER

30 SEPTEMBER

OCTOBER

I open the envelope up and find two train
tickets – to London! 'Oh, wow!'
– *Little Darlings*

1 OCTOBER

2 OCTOBER

3 OCTOBER

4 OCTOBER

OCTOBER

5 OCTOBER

6 OCTOBER

7 OCTOBER

8 OCTOBER

9 OCTOBER

10 OCTOBER

11 OCTOBER

12 OCTOBER

13 OCTOBER

14 OCTOBER

15 OCTOBER

16 OCTOBER

17 OCTOBER

18 OCTOBER

19 OCTOBER

20 OCTOBER

21 OCTOBER

22 OCTOBER

23 OCTOBER

24 OCTOBER

25 OCTOBER

26 OCTOBER

27 OCTOBER

28 OCTOBER

OCTOBER

29 OCTOBER

30 OCTOBER

31 OCTOBER

NOTES

♥ SCRAPBOOK ♥

At the end of any holiday you're sure to have lots of lovely
memories. In these handy scrapbook pages you can stick
photographs, postcards, tickets, anything at all that reminds
you of this summer! It can even be flowers, pebbles
or lolly sticks — whatever is special to you.

♥ SCRAPBOOK ♥

 SCRAPBOOK

♥ SCRAPBOOK ♥

♥ SCRAPBOOK ♥

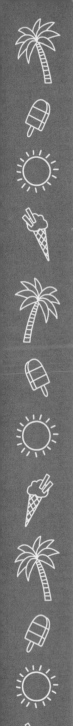

 SCRAPBOOK

♥ SCRAPBOOK ♥

♥ SCRAPBOOK ♥

♥ SCRAPBOOK ♥

♥ SCRAPBOOK ♥

♥ SCRAPBOOK ♥

♥ SCRAPBOOK ♥

♥ SCRAPBOOK ♥

 SCRAPBOOK

♥ SCRAPBOOK ♥

♥ SCRAPBOOK ♥

♥ SCRAPBOOK ♥

food colouring

THE JACQUELINE WILSON HOLIDAY JOURNAL
A DOUBLEDAY BOOK 978 0 857 53096 7

Published in Great Britain by Doubleday,
an imprint of Random House Children's Books
A Random House Group Company

This edition published 2011

1 3 5 7 9 10 8 6 4 2

The Random House Group Limited supports The Forest Stewardship
Council (FSC), the leading international forest certification organisation.
All our titles that are printed on Greenpeace-approved FSC-certified
paper carry the FSC logo. Our paper procurement policy can be
found at www.randomhouse.co.uk/environment.

Set in Blueprint

RANDOM HOUSE CHILDREN'S BOOKS
61–63 Uxbridge Road, London W5 5SA

www.kidsatrandomhouse.co.uk
www.totallyrandombooks.co.uk
www.randomhouse.co.uk

Addresses for companies within The Random House Group Limited
can be found at: www.randomhouse.co.uk/offices.htm

THE RANDOM HOUSE GROUP Limited Reg. No. 954009

A CIP catalogue record for this book is available from the British Library.

Printed and bound in Italy

HOLIDAY QUIZ ANSWERS:

1. Australia 2. Rome 3. Tim 4. Hollywood 5. Mount Everest 6. Germany
7. Euros 8. Lily Cottage 9. Kelly 10. A cake